THEORY
OF SUPPLY

YouTube Mastery: Monetize, Grow, and Thrive as a Content Creator

Table of Contents

Mastering YouTube Monetization: A Comprehensive Guide for Beginners

In the digital age, YouTube has emerged as a powerful platform for content creators to share their passion, connect with a global audience, and, most importantly, generate income. While the prospect of making money on YouTube is enticing, it requires a strategic approach and an understanding of the platform's monetization features. In this comprehensive guide, we'll delve into the essential steps for beginners to master YouTube monetization.

Understanding YouTube's Partner Program

The first and foremost step towards monetizing your YouTube channel is to join the YouTube Partner Program (YPP). To be eligible, your channel must have at least 1,000 subscribers and 4,000 watch hours in the last 12 months. Once accepted, you can start earning money through ads displayed on your videos.

Creating Quality Content

Quality content is the backbone of any successful YouTube channel. Consistently produce engaging, informative, and entertaining videos that cater to your target audience. Higher-quality content tends to attract more views and, consequently, increases your potential for earning revenue through ads.

Leveraging Ad Revenue

With the YouTube Partner Program, you gain access to ad revenue. YouTube places ads on your videos, and you earn a share of the revenue generated from those ads. Understanding the different types of ads, such as skippable ads, non-skippable ads, and display ads, can help you optimize your revenue potential.

Exploring Super Chats and Channel Memberships

Super Chats and Channel Memberships are additional ways to monetize your channel. Super Chats allow viewers to pay to have their messages highlighted during live streams, while Channel Memberships enable fans to subscribe to your channel for exclusive perks. These features deepen your connection with your audience while providing an extra income stream.

Diversifying with Affiliate Marketing

Beyond YouTube's built-in monetization features, consider diversifying your income with affiliate marketing. Partner with brands and promote their products or services in your video descriptions. Earn commissions for every sale or lead generated through your unique affiliate links.

Unlocking the Power of Sponsorships

Collaborating with brands for sponsored content can significantly boost your revenue. As your channel grows, brands may approach you for partnerships. Alternatively, you can proactively reach out to relevant brands within your niche to explore potential sponsorships.

Tapping into Merchandise Sales

Creating and selling merchandise related to your channel can be a lucrative venture. From branded T-shirts to custom accessories, merchandise sales allow your audience to support you while proudly displaying their affiliation with your content.

Maximizing Revenue through YouTube Premium

YouTube Premium subscribers pay a monthly fee for an ad-free experience. As a content creator, you receive a share of the revenue generated from Premium subscribers who watch your content. This additional revenue stream can contribute significantly to your overall earnings.

Building an Email List for Direct Outreach

While not directly tied to YouTube, building an email list is a powerful way to engage with your audience outside of the platform. Use email marketing to promote your products, services, or exclusive content, creating another avenue for income.

Engaging with Your Community

Building a loyal and engaged community is crucial for sustained success on YouTube. Respond to comments, participate in live chats, and foster a sense of belonging among your audience. A dedicated community is more likely to support you through various monetization channels.

Conclusion

Mastering YouTube monetization as a beginner requires a combination of dedication, quality content creation, and strategic planning. By understanding and leveraging YouTube's built-in features, exploring external opportunities like affiliate marketing and sponsorships, and fostering a strong community, you can create a sustainable income stream while doing what you love. Remember, success on YouTube is a journey, and as you grow, so will your opportunities to monetize your passion for creating content.

Creative Ways to Monetize Your YouTube Channel Beyond Ad Revenue

YouTube's Partner Program provides a gateway for creators to earn revenue through ads, but there's a world of untapped potential beyond traditional ad earnings. In this article, we'll explore creative and diversified strategies to monetize your YouTube channel, allowing you to maximize your income while engaging your audience in unique ways.

1. Affiliate Marketing Adventures:

Partner with brands relevant to your niche and include affiliate links in your video descriptions. Earn commissions for every sale generated through your unique links, transforming your recommendations into revenue.

2. Unlocking the Treasure Chest of Merchandise:

Design and sell branded merchandise that resonates with your audience. From T-shirts and mugs to custom accessories, merchandise sales not only generate income but also strengthen your community's connection with your brand.

3. Exclusive Content via Memberships:

Introduce channel memberships for exclusive perks like early access, custom badges, and members-only content. Your most dedicated fans can subscribe, providing a steady income stream while fostering a sense of belonging within your community.

4. Virtual Events and Webinars:

Host virtual events, workshops, or webinars related to your channel's content. Charge a fee for access, offering your audience an immersive experience and providing you with an additional income stream.

5. Crowdfunding Creativity:

Platforms like Patreon allow your audience to support you directly. Offer exclusive content, behind-the-scenes access, or personalized shoutouts to patrons, turning your most dedicated followers into active financial supporters.

6. Skill Sharing with Online Courses:

Share your expertise by creating and selling online courses. Platforms like Udemy or Teachable provide opportunities to monetize your knowledge, turning your YouTube channel into a gateway for deeper learning.

7. Innovative Sponsorship Collaborations:

Go beyond traditional sponsorships by collaborating with brands in unique ways. Integrating sponsored challenges, storytelling, or interactive content can provide value to both your audience and the sponsoring brand.

8. Fan-Funded Projects:

Engage your audience in fan-funded projects. Crowdfunding platforms like Kickstarter or Indiegogo can support your ambitious ventures, allowing your community to actively contribute to the creation of new and exciting content.

9. Digital Products and Printables:

Create and sell digital products or printables related to your content. This could include e-books, digital art, or printable resources that cater to your audience's interests, providing an additional revenue stream.

10. Consultation and Services:

If your channel revolves around a specific skill or expertise, offer consultation services. This could range from one-on-one coaching sessions to personalized advice, allowing you to monetize your knowledge and connect with your audience on a deeper level.

Conclusion:

Diversifying your income streams is key to building a sustainable and profitable YouTube channel. By exploring these creative monetization strategies, you not only increase your financial stability but also enhance your connection with your audience. As you embark on this monetization journey, remember that authenticity and value creation are the pillars that will sustain both your channel and your income streams in the long run.

Building a Profitable YouTube Channel: Strategies for Content Creators

Creating a successful and profitable YouTube channel requires more than just uploading videos. It demands a strategic approach, consistent effort, and a deep understanding of your audience. In this article, we'll explore key strategies for content creators looking to turn their passion into a sustainable source of income.

1. Define Your Niche:

Identify a specific niche that aligns with your interests and expertise. A well-defined niche not only helps you target a specific audience but also makes it easier for advertisers and sponsors to collaborate with you.

2. Know Your Audience:

Understand your audience's preferences, demographics, and interests. Regularly engage with your viewers through comments, polls, and surveys to tailor your content to their needs and keep them invested in your channel.

3. Consistency is Key:

Establish a consistent uploading schedule. Regular content keeps your audience engaged and helps with algorithmic favorability, increasing the likelihood of your videos being recommended to a wider audience.

4. Optimize for Search (SEO):

Master the art of Search Engine Optimization (SEO) for YouTube. Use relevant keywords in your video titles, descriptions, and tags to enhance discoverability and increase the chances of appearing in search results.

5. Quality Over Quantity:

Prioritize quality content over quantity. High-quality videos that provide value, entertain, or educate will attract and retain viewers, ultimately contributing to higher ad revenue and more opportunities for monetization.

6. Create Click-Worthy Thumbnails and Titles:

Thumbnails and titles are the first things viewers notice. Craft compelling and click-worthy thumbnails and titles that accurately represent your content and entice users to click and watch.

7. Engage Your Community:

Cultivate an active and engaged community by responding to comments, asking for feedback, and incorporating viewer suggestions. A loyal audience is more likely to support you through various monetization channels.

8. Diversify Monetization Streams:

Beyond ad revenue, explore additional revenue streams like affiliate marketing, merchandise sales, and sponsored content. Diversifying your income helps create a more stable financial foundation for your channel.

9. Collaborate and Cross-Promote:

Collaborate with other YouTubers in your niche to expand your reach. Cross-promotion introduces your channel to new audiences, fostering growth and increasing opportunities for monetization.

10. Utilize Analytics for Strategy Refinement

Regularly analyze your YouTube Analytics to understand which content performs well and why. Use this data to refine your content strategy, identify trends, and adapt to the evolving preferences of your audience.

Conclusion:

Building a profitable YouTube channel is a journey that requires dedication, adaptability, and a deep connection with your audience. By defining your niche, consistently delivering high-quality content, engaging with your community, and diversifying your monetization streams, you can transform your passion into a sustainable source of income. Remember, the key is not only to create content but to build a brand and a community that stands the test of time.

Unlocking Passive Income on YouTube: Diversifying Revenue Streams

YouTube's allure goes beyond fame and ad revenue – it's a platform that can be leveraged for creating passive income streams. In this article, we'll explore strategies for content creators to unlock passive income on YouTube by diversifying revenue streams and building a more resilient financial foundation.

1. Affiliate Marketing Automation:

Implement evergreen affiliate marketing strategies by creating videos with content that stays relevant over time. Embed affiliate links strategically, allowing you to earn commissions on product sales long after the video's initial release.

2. Create Evergreen Content:

Develop timeless content that remains relevant to your audience over an extended period. Evergreen videos have a longer shelf life, continuing to attract views and generate ad revenue, affiliate sales, and other income sources passively.

3. Invest in Automation Tools:

Utilize automation tools for social media promotion, audience engagement, and content scheduling. By automating repetitive tasks, you free up time to focus on creating new content while maintaining a consistent presence across platforms.

4. Build a Membership Community:

Establish a membership community that provides exclusive perks to subscribers. While this requires initial effort, once set up, it offers a recurring income stream as members continue to pay for exclusive content and benefits.

5. License Your Content:

Explore licensing opportunities for your content. Platforms, businesses, or individuals may be interested in using your videos, and licensing agreements can provide a steady stream of passive income.

6. Create and Sell Digital Products:

Develop digital products such as eBooks, presets, or templates related to your niche. Once created, these products can be sold passively, generating income without ongoing time and effort.

7. Optimize Your Video Library:

Regularly revisit and optimize your existing video library. Update video descriptions, tags, and thumbnails to enhance their visibility in search results, attracting new viewers and passive income opportunities.

8. Implement Ad Revenue Optimization:

Maximize ad revenue through strategic ad placements, mid-roll ads, and optimizing your video length. Longer videos tend to generate more ad revenue, providing a passive income boost over time.

9. Explore Royalty-Free Music and Stock Footage:

Create and sell royalty-free music or stock footage libraries. As creators and businesses search for high-quality assets, your content can become a passive income source through licensing agreements.

10. Set Up a Merchandise Store:

Develop and set up an online merchandise store. Once configured, your audience can purchase branded products passively, providing you with a continuous income stream without direct involvement.

Conclusion:

Unlocking passive income on YouTube involves strategic planning, diversification, and a focus on creating evergreen content. By incorporating affiliate marketing, building a membership community, licensing your content, and exploring various passive income avenues, you can transform your YouTube channel into a sustainable source of income that continues to grow over time. Remember, the key to unlocking passive income lies in building a foundation that allows you to earn even when you're not actively creating new content.

YouTube Affiliate Marketing: Turn Views into Cash

YouTube is not only a platform for content creation but also a lucrative space for affiliate marketing. By strategically integrating affiliate marketing into your videos, you can turn views into a substantial revenue stream. In this article, we'll explore how content creators can harness the power of YouTube affiliate marketing to monetize their content effectively.

1. Choose Relevant Affiliate Programs:

Align with affiliate programs that resonate with your audience and niche. Select products or services that genuinely provide value, as authenticity is key to building trust with your viewers.

2. Integrate Affiliate Links Naturally:

Seamlessly incorporate affiliate links into your video content. Whether through product reviews, tutorials, or recommendations, make the links a natural extension of your content to encourage clicks.

3. Craft Compelling Call-to-Actions:

Motivate your audience to take action by including persuasive calls-to-action (CTAs). Clearly communicate the benefits of the affiliated products or services and encourage viewers to use your unique affiliate links.

4. Disclose Affiliation Transparently:

Transparency builds trust. Clearly disclose your affiliation with the products or services you promote. Open communication about your use of affiliate links fosters a trustworthy relationship with your audience.

5. Leverage Tracking and Analytics:

Use tracking tools provided by affiliate programs to monitor the performance of your links. Analyze data to understand which products resonate most with your audience, allowing you to refine your marketing strategy.

6. Create Dedicated Affiliate Content:

Develop content specifically designed around affiliate marketing. This could include in-depth reviews, comparison videos, or tutorials showcasing the benefits of the products or services you're promoting.

7. Utilize YouTube Cards and End Screens:

Maximize the visibility of your affiliate links by incorporating YouTube Cards and End Screens. These features allow you to direct viewers to external links seamlessly, increasing the likelihood of conversions.

8. Negotiate Exclusive Discounts for Your Audience:

Work with affiliate partners to negotiate exclusive discounts or promotions for your audience. Exclusive offers can incentivize viewers to use your affiliate links, enhancing conversion rates.

9. Stay Authentic and Genuine:

Avoid over-promotion and prioritize authenticity. Recommending products you genuinely believe in and explaining how they've benefited you can establish a more sincere connection with your audience.

10. Test and Optimize Strategies:

Continuously experiment with different affiliate marketing strategies. Test various types of content, CTAs, and promotional approaches to identify what resonates best with your audience, and refine your methods accordingly.

Conclusion:

YouTube affiliate marketing is a powerful tool for content creators to monetize their videos and turn views into a consistent revenue stream. By selecting relevant affiliate programs, integrating links naturally, and staying authentic, you can create a symbiotic relationship between your content and affiliate marketing efforts. As you refine your strategies and build trust with your audience, the potential for earning substantial income through affiliate marketing on YouTube becomes even more promising.

Monetizing Your Expertise: Creating Online Courses on YouTube

YouTube isn't just a platform for sharing knowledge; it can also serve as a gateway to monetize your expertise through online courses. In this article, we'll explore how content creators can leverage YouTube to create and sell online courses, turning their knowledge into a profitable venture.

1. Identify Your Niche and Expertise:

Pinpoint a specific niche within your expertise. Clearly define what you're passionate about and where your expertise lies. This focused approach will attract a more targeted audience interested in your course offerings.

2. Build Credibility Through YouTube Content:

Establish yourself as an authority in your field by consistently creating high-quality YouTube content. Share valuable insights, tips, and tutorials that showcase your expertise, building trust with your audience.

3. Understand Your Audience's Needs:

Conduct research to understand your audience's pain points and learning needs. Tailor your online courses to address these specific challenges, ensuring that your content provides practical solutions and tangible value.

4. Create Teaser Content on YouTube:

Develop teaser content on YouTube to give viewers a glimpse of what your courses offer. Showcase your teaching style, the depth of your knowledge, and the potential benefits of enrolling in your online courses.

5. Choose the Right Online Course Platform:

Select a reliable online course platform to host and sell your courses. Platforms like Udemy, Teachable, or Thinkific provide user-friendly interfaces and built-in tools for marketing and selling your educational content.

6. Integrate YouTube with Your Course:

Integrate your YouTube channel with your online course platform. Use YouTube to drive traffic to your course landing pages, leveraging the existing audience and visibility you've built on the platform.

7. Offer Value through Free and Premium Content:

Strike a balance between free content on YouTube and premium content within your courses. Offer valuable insights and guidance for free, while enticing viewers to enroll in your courses for more in-depth, specialized knowledge.

8. Engage with Your Community:

Foster engagement and a sense of community among your audience. Respond to comments on YouTube, create discussion forums within your courses, and encourage peer-to-peer interaction. A thriving community enhances the overall learning experience.

9. Leverage Live Q&A Sessions:

Host live Q&A sessions on YouTube to address questions related to your expertise. Use these sessions to promote your online courses and provide additional value, creating a direct connection with your audience.

10. Promote Your Courses Strategically:

Develop a strategic promotional plan for your courses. Utilize YouTube's promotional features, social media, and email marketing to create awareness about your offerings and drive enrollments.

Conclusion:

Monetizing your expertise through online courses on YouTube is not just a financial venture but a way to empower others with your knowledge. By carefully crafting your niche, building credibility on YouTube, and strategically integrating online courses, you can create a sustainable income stream while making a meaningful impact in your field. As you embark on this journey, remember that the key lies in delivering valuable content that resonates with your audience and addresses their learning needs.

The Art of Sponsored Content: Monetizing Your Channel with Brand Collaborations

Sponsored content presents a unique opportunity for content creators to monetize their YouTube channels while maintaining authenticity and providing value to their audience. In this article, we'll delve into the art of sponsored content, exploring strategies for effectively collaborating with brands and maximizing the financial potential of your channel.

1. Align with Brands Relevant to Your Niche:

Choose brands that align seamlessly with your content and resonate with your audience. Authenticity is crucial in sponsored content, and partnering with brands that fit your niche enhances the overall viewer experience.

2. Build Credibility Before Pursuing Sponsorships:

Establish a credible and engaged audience before actively pursuing brand collaborations. Brands are more likely to invest in content creators with a dedicated following and a track record of delivering quality content.

3. Create a Professional Media Kit:

Develop a professional media kit showcasing your channel statistics, demographics, and the value you can provide to potential sponsors.

A well-crafted media kit serves as a powerful tool when approaching brands for collaborations.

4. Disclose Sponsored Content Transparently:

Transparency is key to maintaining trust with your audience. Clearly disclose sponsored content at the beginning of your videos or in the video description. Open communication ensures authenticity and honesty.

5. Integrate Brand Messaging Seamlessly:

Weave the brand's messaging seamlessly into your content. Avoid making the sponsorship feel forced or unnatural. The more organically the brand fits into your narrative, the more positively it will be received by your audience.

6. Negotiate Fair Compensation:

Know your worth and negotiate fair compensation for your sponsored content. Consider factors such as your audience size, engagement rates, and the level of effort required for the collaboration. Don't undersell your influence.

7. Prioritize Long-Term Relationships:

Foster long-term relationships with brands rather than one-off collaborations. Consistent partnerships with the same brands can lead to more significant financial rewards and create a sense of continuity for your audience.

8. Maintain Creative Control:

Ensure that you retain creative control over your content. Collaborate with brands that respect your creative vision and allow you to incorporate their messaging in a way that feels authentic to your style and tone.

9. Showcase Successful Collaborations:

Highlight successful brand collaborations in your portfolio. Showcase the positive outcomes and engagement generated from previous sponsorships to attract more brands interested in partnering with an influential content creator.

10. Diversify Collaboration Types:

Explore various collaboration types beyond product placements, such as sponsored giveaways, sponsored challenges, or co-created content. Diversifying collaboration types keeps your content fresh and engaging.

Conclusion:

The art of sponsored content involves a delicate balance between monetization and maintaining the trust of your audience. By strategically selecting brands, prioritizing transparency, negotiating fair compensation, and showcasing successful collaborations, you can turn brand collaborations into a sustainable source of income while enriching your content and audience experience. Remember, the key lies in finding harmony between brand partnerships and the authentic voice that has made your channel successful in the first place.

Crowdfunding Success on YouTube: Funding Your Projects with Fans

Crowdfunding has become a powerful avenue for content creators to bring their projects to life while fostering a deeper connection with their audience. In this article, we'll explore strategies for achieving crowdfunding success on YouTube, leveraging the support of your fans to fund and realize your creative endeavors.

1. Define Clear Project Goals:

Clearly articulate the goals of your project. Whether it's creating a new series, producing high-quality videos, or launching a special event, transparently communicate the purpose and expected outcomes to your audience.

2. Select the Right Crowdfunding Platform:

Choose a crowdfunding platform that aligns with your project and audience. Platforms like Kickstarter, Indiegogo, or Patreon offer different models of crowdfunding, allowing you to tailor your approach based on your project's nature.

3. Create Compelling Campaign Content:

Develop a compelling and visually appealing campaign video. Clearly express your passion for the project, outline how the funds will be utilized, and highlight the exclusive perks supporters will receive. Make it a story that resonates emotionally.

4. Set Realistic Funding Targets:

Set achievable funding targets based on the scope of your project. Realistic goals not only make your campaign more attainable but also instill confidence in your audience that their contributions will have a meaningful impact.

5. Offer Irresistible Rewards:

Craft enticing and exclusive rewards for your backers. Consider personalized shoutouts, behind-the-scenes access, or limited-edition merchandise. The more valuable and unique the rewards, the more likely fans will be motivated to contribute.

6. Leverage YouTube for Campaign Promotion:

Utilize your YouTube channel to promote your crowdfunding campaign. Create dedicated videos discussing the project, its goals, and the perks of contributing. Regularly update your audience on the campaign's progress to maintain momentum.

7. Host Live Q&A Sessions:

Engage with your audience through live Q&A sessions dedicated to your crowdfunding campaign. Answer questions, provide additional details about the project, and encourage viewers to participate by contributing or sharing the campaign.

8. Build a Sense of Community:

Foster a sense of community around your project. Encourage backers and potential supporters to share their thoughts, ideas, and excitement about the project. A vibrant community not only boosts morale but can attract more contributors.

9. Provide Regular Updates:

Keep your audience informed with regular updates. Share progress, milestones achieved, and any adjustments to the project plan. Transparent communication enhances trust and reinforces your commitment to delivering on your promises.

10. Express Gratitude and Recognition:

Show gratitude to your backers and recognize their contributions. Dedicate segments of your content to thanking supporters, featuring their names or messages in videos, and making them feel an integral part of the project's success.

Conclusion:

Crowdfunding success on YouTube is about more than just funding; it's a collaborative journey with your audience. By setting clear goals, leveraging the right crowdfunding platform, creating compelling content, and nurturing a supportive community, you can fund your projects with the backing of your dedicated fans. Ultimately, the success of crowdfunding goes beyond financial support; it's about building a stronger bond with your audience as they actively contribute to bringing your creative visions to life.

Turning Views into Sales: Effective Merchandise Strategies for YouTubers

Monetizing your YouTube channel goes beyond ad revenue; it extends to creating and selling merchandise that resonates with your audience. In this article, we'll explore strategies for YouTubers to effectively turn views into sales by leveraging merchandise as a supplementary income stream.

1. Understand Your Audience's Preferences:

Conduct surveys or engage with your audience to understand their preferences. Tailor your merchandise to align with their interests, ensuring that your products resonate with the community you've built.

2. Design Merchandise that Reflects Your Brand:

Create merchandise that reflects your unique brand and style. Whether it's catchy slogans, memorable catchphrases, or personalized artwork, the merchandise should be an extension of your content and identity.

3. Start with a Few Signature Products:

Begin with a few signature products to test the waters. Focus on items that are likely to have broad appeal, such as T-shirts, stickers, or mugs. As you gauge interest, you can expand your merchandise line accordingly.

4. Collaborate with Professional Designers:

If design isn't your forte, collaborate with professional designers to create visually appealing merchandise. Investing in high-quality designs enhances the perceived value of your products and increases the likelihood of sales.

5. Promote Merchandise in Your Videos:

Actively promote your merchandise in your videos. Showcase the products, explain their significance, and provide a compelling call-to-action for viewers to check out your merchandise store. Utilize YouTube Cards and End Screens for easy navigation.

6. Limited Edition and Exclusive Drops:

Create a sense of urgency and exclusivity by introducing limited edition or exclusive merchandise drops. This strategy encourages fans to make a purchase promptly to secure unique items, driving sales during specific periods.

7. Run Contests and Giveaways:

Generate excitement around your merchandise by running contests and giveaways. Encourage participation through engagement metrics, such as likes, comments, or shares, and reward winners with your exclusive products.

8. Utilize Social Media for Promotion:

Leverage your social media platforms to promote your merchandise. Share engaging visuals, testimonials from happy customers, and updates on new product releases. Social media provides an additional channel to reach potential buyers.

9. Bundle Deals and Discounts:

Encourage larger purchases by offering bundle deals or discounts for buying multiple items. Bundling related merchandise or providing limited-time discounts can incentivize viewers to grab more than one item from your store.

10. Collect and Showcase Fan Photos:

Encourage fans to share photos of themselves with your merchandise. Showcase these fan photos on your social media and in your videos. The social proof generated by happy customers can influence others to make a purchase.

Conclusion:

Effectively turning views into merchandise sales requires a thoughtful approach that aligns with your brand and engages your audience. By understanding your audience, designing appealing products, promoting strategically in your videos, and utilizing various promotional tactics, you can create a successful merchandise strategy that not only generates revenue but also strengthens the connection with your fanbase. Remember, the key is to offer products that fans are proud to associate with your brand.

YouTube SEO for Profit: Optimizing Your Videos to Boost Revenue

In the competitive landscape of YouTube, mastering Search Engine Optimization (SEO) is crucial for maximizing visibility and, consequently, revenue. In this article, we'll explore strategies for content creators to optimize their videos effectively, turning YouTube SEO into a powerful tool for boosting income.

1. Thorough Keyword Research:

Conduct thorough keyword research to identify relevant and high-search-volume terms within your niche. Incorporate these keywords naturally into your video titles, descriptions, and tags to enhance discoverability.

2. Create Compelling Thumbnails:

Craft compelling and visually appealing thumbnails. Thumbnails play a significant role in attracting clicks, so use vibrant visuals, readable text, and images that spark curiosity to entice viewers to click on your videos.

3. Engaging Video Descriptions:

Write detailed and engaging video descriptions. Include relevant keywords naturally and provide additional context about your video. A well-crafted description not only aids in SEO but also encourages viewer engagement.

4. Utilize Closed Captions (CC):

Enable closed captions for your videos. This not only improves accessibility but also provides YouTube with additional textual content to understand the context of your videos, boosting your SEO efforts.

5. Optimize Video Length:

Pay attention to your video length. While it's important to keep viewers engaged, longer videos tend to perform better in terms of ad revenue. Strike a balance by creating content that retains viewer interest throughout.

6. Encourage Viewer Engagement:

Actively encourage viewer engagement through likes, comments, and shares. High engagement metrics signal to YouTube that your content is valuable, contributing to higher rankings and increased visibility.

7. Consistent Upload Schedule:

Establish a consistent upload schedule. Regular uploads not only keep your audience engaged but also signal to YouTube's algorithm that your channel is active, potentially boosting your videos in search results.

8. Utilize YouTube Playlists:

Create playlists for your videos. Organizing your content into playlists can improve watch time and keep viewers on your channel longer, positively impacting your video and channel rankings.

9. Promote Watch Time:

Prioritize watch time, a critical metric for YouTube's algorithm. Engaging, longer videos that keep viewers on the platform contribute to higher ad revenue and improved search rankings.

10. Monitor Analytics and Refine Strategy:

Regularly monitor YouTube Analytics to understand how your videos are performing. Identify trends, assess viewer behavior, and refine your SEO strategy based on the insights gained.

Conclusion:

Optimizing your YouTube videos for SEO is not just about gaining visibility; it's a strategic approach to boost revenue and build a sustainable channel. By incorporating effective keyword research, creating compelling thumbnails and video descriptions, and prioritizing engagement and watch time, you can enhance your videos' discoverability and increase your potential for ad revenue and other monetization avenues on YouTube. Stay proactive, adapt to changing trends, and continually refine your SEO strategy to keep your channel on the path to profitability.

www.ingramcontent.com/pod-product-compliance
Lightning Source LLC
LaVergne TN
LVHW022126060326
832903LV00063B/4788